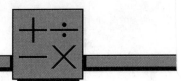

Table Of Contents

Glossary

Angle. Two rays with the same end point.

Area. The number of square units needed to cover a region.

Centimeter. A metric system measurement. There are 2.54 centimeters in·an inch.

Cup (c.). A unit of volume in the customary system equal to 8 ounces.

Decimal. A number with one or more places to the right of a decimal point, such as 6.5 or 2.25.

Denominator. The number below the fraction bar in a fraction.

Diameter. A line segment that passes through the center of a circle and has both end points on the circle.

Digit. The symbols used to write numbers: 0, 1, 2, 3, 4, 5, 6, 7, 8, and 9.

Dividend. The larger number that is divided by the smaller number, or divisor, in a division problem. In the problem 28 ÷ 7 = 4, 28 is the dividend.

Divisor. The number that is divided into the dividend in a division problem. In the problem 28 ÷ 7 = 4, 7 is the divisor.

Equivalent Fractions. Fractions that name the same number.

Estimate. To give an approximate rather than an exact answer.

Factor. The numbers multiplied together in a multiplication problem.

Fraction. A number that names part of a whole, such as 1/2 or 1/3.

Kilometer (km). A unit of length. There are 1000 meters in a kilometer.

Liter (L). A unit in the metric system used to measure amounts of liquid.

Meter (m). A unit of length in the metric system. A meter is equal to 39.37 inches.

Mile (mi.). A mile is equal to 1760 yards.

Mixed Numeral. A number written as a whole number and a fraction.

Multiple. The product of a specific number and any other number. For example, the multiples of 2 are 2 (2 x 1), 4 (2 x 2), 6, 8, 10, 12, and so on.

Numerator. The number above the fraction bar in a fraction.

Octagon. A polygon with eight sides.

Ordered Pair. A pair of numbers used to locate a point in a plane.

Pentagon. A polygon with five sides.

Perimeter. The distance around an object. Found by adding the lengths of the sides.

Pint (pt). A unit of volume in the customary system equal to 2 cups.

Polygon. A closed plane figure with straight sides called line segments.

Product. The answer of a multiplication problem.

Quart (qt). A unit of volume equal to four cups or two pints.

Quotient. The answer of a division problem.

Radius. A line segment with one endpoint on the circle and the other end point at the center.

Rectangle. A figure with four corners and four sides. Sides opposite each other are the same length.

Regroup. To use one ten to form ten ones, one 100 to form ten tens, fifteen ones to form one ten and five ones, and so on.

Remainder. The number left over in the quotient of a division problem.

Rounding. Expressing a number to the nearest ten, hundred, thousand, and so on. For example, round 18 up to 20; round 11 down to 10.

Sequencing. Putting numbers in the correct order, such as 7, 8, 9.

Square. A figure with four corners and four sides of the same length.

Triangle. A figure with three corners and three sides.

Yard. A measurement of distance in the customary system. There are three feet in a yard.

Place Value

Place value is the value of a digit, or numeral, shown by where it is in the number. For example, in the number 1234, 1 has the place value of thousands, 2 is hundreds, 3 is tens, and 4 is ones.

Directions: Put the numbers in the correct boxes to find how far the car has traveled.

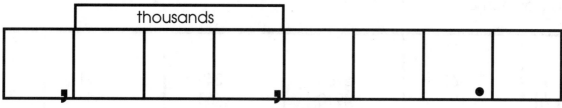

one thousand
six hundreds
eight ones
nine ten thousands
four tens
two millions
seven tenths
five hundred thousands

How many miles has the car traveled? _____

Directions:

In the number:

2386	_____ is in the ones place.
4957	_____ is in the hundreds place.
102,432	_____ is in the ten thousands place.
489,753	_____ is in the one thousands place.
1,743,998	_____ is in the millions place.
9,301,671	_____ is in the hundred thousands place.
7,521,834	_____ is in the tens place.

Name: _____

Addition

Addition is "putting together" or adding two or more numbers to find the sum. Regrouping is to use one ten to form ten ones, one 100 to form ten tens, fifteen ones to form one ten and five ones, and so on.

Directions: Add using regrouping. Color in all of the boxes with a 5 in the answer to help the dog find its way home.

	63 +22	5268 4910 +1683	248 +463	291 +543	2934 +112
1736 +5367	2946 +7384	3245 1239 +981	738 +692	896 +729	594 +738
2603 +5004	4507 +289	1483 +6753	1258 +6301	27 469 +6002	4637 +7531
782 +65	485 +276	3421 +8064			
48 93 +26	90 263 +864	362 453 +800			

Subtraction

Subtraction is "taking away" or subtracting one number from another. Regrouping is to use one ten to form ten ones, one 100 to form ten tens, fifteen ones to form one ten and five ones, and so on.

Directions: Subtract using regrouping.

Examples:

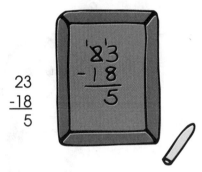

$$
\begin{array}{r} 23 \\ -18 \\ \hline 5 \end{array}
$$

$$
\begin{array}{r} 243 \\ -96 \\ \hline 147 \end{array}
$$

$$
\begin{array}{r} 81 \\ -53 \\ \hline \end{array}
\qquad
\begin{array}{r} 76 \\ -49 \\ \hline \end{array}
\qquad
\begin{array}{r} 94 \\ -38 \\ \hline \end{array}
\qquad
\begin{array}{r} 156 \\ -77 \\ \hline \end{array}
\qquad
\begin{array}{r} 243 \\ -29 \\ \hline \end{array}
\qquad
\begin{array}{r} 468 \\ -293 \\ \hline \end{array}
$$

$$
\begin{array}{r} 341 \\ -83 \\ \hline \end{array}
\qquad
\begin{array}{r} 568 \\ -173 \\ \hline \end{array}
\qquad
\begin{array}{r} 806 \\ -738 \\ \hline \end{array}
\qquad
\begin{array}{r} 647 \\ -289 \\ \hline \end{array}
\qquad
\begin{array}{r} 730 \\ -518 \\ \hline \end{array}
\qquad
\begin{array}{r} 961 \\ -846 \\ \hline \end{array}
$$

$$
\begin{array}{r} 573 \\ -76 \\ \hline \end{array}
\qquad
\begin{array}{r} 604 \\ -55 \\ \hline \end{array}
\qquad
\begin{array}{r} 254 \\ -69 \\ \hline \end{array}
\qquad
\begin{array}{r} 111 \\ -82 \\ \hline \end{array}
\qquad
\begin{array}{r} 358 \\ -99 \\ \hline \end{array}
\qquad
\begin{array}{r} 147 \\ -49 \\ \hline \end{array}
$$

$$
\begin{array}{r} 265 \\ -19 \\ \hline \end{array}
\qquad
\begin{array}{r} 372 \\ -59 \\ \hline \end{array}
\qquad
\begin{array}{r} 180 \\ -106 \\ \hline \end{array}
\qquad
\begin{array}{r} 325 \\ -68 \\ \hline \end{array}
\qquad
\begin{array}{r} 873 \\ -35 \\ \hline \end{array}
\qquad
\begin{array}{r} 726 \\ -29 \\ \hline \end{array}
$$

Name: _____

Rounding

Rounding a number means expressing it to the nearest ten, hundred, thousand, and so on.

Directions: Round the following numbers to the nearest ten. If the number has 5 ones or more, round it up to the next highest ten. For example, round 26 up to 30. If the number has 4 ones or less, round down to the nearest ten, such as rounding 44 down to 40.

18 _____   33 _____   82 _____   56 _____

24 _____   49 _____   91 _____   67 _____

Directions: Round to the nearest hundred. If 5 tens or more, round up. If 4 tens or less, round down.

243 _____   689 _____   263 _____   162 _____

389 _____   720 _____   351 _____   490 _____

463 _____   846 _____   928 _____   733 _____

Directions: Round to the nearest thousand. If number has 5 hundreds or more, round up. If 4 hundreds or less, round down.

2638 _____   3940 _____   8653 _____   6238 _____

1429 _____   5061 _____   7289 _____   2742 _____

9460 _____   3109 _____   4697 _____   8302 _____

Directions: Round to the nearest ten thousand. If the number has 5 thousands or more, round up. If 4 thousands or less, round down.

11,368 _____   38,421 _____   75,302 _____   67,932 _____

14,569 _____   49,926 _____   93,694 _____   81,648 _____

26,784 _____   87,065 _____   57,843 _____   29,399 _____

Name: _____

Addition And Subtraction

Addition is "putting together" or adding two or more numbers to find the sum. Subtraction is "taking away" or subtracting one number from another.

Regrouping is to use one ten to form ten ones, one 100 to form ten tens, fifteen ones to form one ten and five ones, and so on.

Directions: Add or subtract. Remember to regroup.

```
  32        183        456        643
  68        246        398       -377
 +43        +89       +597
```

```
1563       3586       8711       9361       5734
-941       +4218     -4937      -7452      +6298
```

```
 293        743        849       1227       9117
 431       -529        250       2431      -3828
 +93                   +82      +5792
```

68 + 93 + 146 = _____   73 + 246 + 1579 = _____

43 + 745 - 29 = _____   128 + 403 + 2571= _____

156 + 627 + 541 = _____   97 + 51 + 37 + 79 = _____

Tom walks 389 steps from his house to the video store. It is 149 steps to Elm Street. It is 52 steps from Maple Street to the video store. How many steps is it from Elm Street to Maple Steet?

_____

Name: _____

Addition And Subtraction

Addition is "putting together" or adding two or more numbers to find the sum. Subtraction is "taking away" or subtracting one number from another.

Directions: Add or subtract.

$$
\begin{array}{r} 38 \\ 43 \\ +21 \\ \hline \end{array}
\qquad
\begin{array}{r} 1269 \\ 2453 \\ +8219 \\ \hline \end{array}
\qquad
\begin{array}{r} 5792 \\ -4814 \\ \hline \end{array}
\qquad
\begin{array}{r} 629 \\ 491 \\ +308 \\ \hline \end{array}
\qquad
\begin{array}{r} 4697 \\ -2988 \\ \hline \end{array}
$$

$$
\begin{array}{r} 5280 \\ -3147 \\ \hline \end{array}
\qquad
\begin{array}{r} 68 \\ 27 \\ +42 \\ \hline \end{array}
\qquad
\begin{array}{r} 197 \\ 436 \\ +213 \\ \hline \end{array}
\qquad
\begin{array}{r} 7321 \\ -2789 \\ \hline \end{array}
\qquad
\begin{array}{r} 456 \\ +974 \\ \hline \end{array}
$$

$$
\begin{array}{r} 3932 \\ +4681 \\ \hline \end{array}
\qquad
\begin{array}{r} 492 \\ 863 \\ +57 \\ \hline \end{array}
\qquad
\begin{array}{r} 9873 \\ +5483 \\ \hline \end{array}
\qquad
\begin{array}{r} 4978 \\ +2131 \\ \hline \end{array}
\qquad
\begin{array}{r} 6235 \\ +2986 \\ \hline \end{array}
$$

Sue stocked her pond with 263 bass and 187 trout. The turtles ate 97 fish. How many fish are left? _____

Name: _____

Multiples

A multiple is the product of a specific number and any other number. For example, the multiples of 2 are 2 (2 x 1) 4, (2 x 2), 6, 8, 10, 12, and so on.

Directions: Write the missing multiples.

Example: Count by fives.
5, 10, 15, 20, 25, 30, 35. These are multiples of 5.

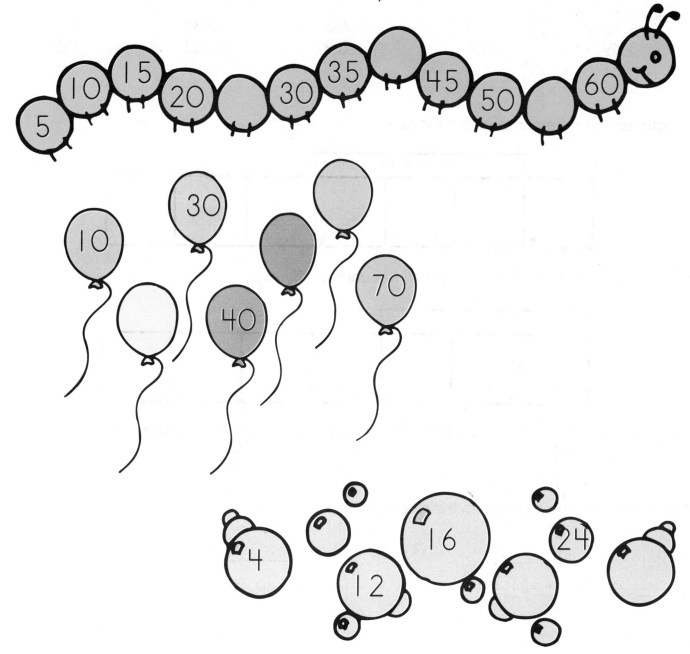

Name: _____

Review

Directions: Add or subtract using regrouping.

67	5029	732	2467	8453
93	-3068	801	+3184	-6087
+48		+18		

5792	7489	463	3537	6342
-3889	+5938	-209	-2394	+959

Directions: Write the numbers in the boxes.

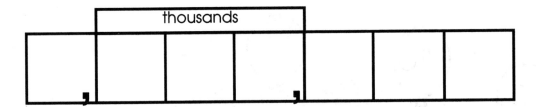

eight million, four hundred thousand, nine hundred fifty two

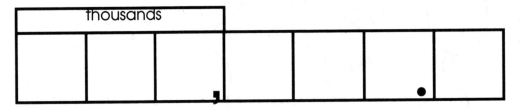

five hundred thousands, three ten thousands, five thousands, zero hundreds, four tens, one one, two tenths

Directions: Fill in the blanks with the missing multiples.

6, 12, 18, _____, 30, _____   3, _____, _____, 12, 15

4, _____, 12, 16, _____, 24   _____, 10, 15, _____, _____

Name: _____

Multiplication

Multiplication is a short way to find the sum of adding the same number a certain amount of times, such as 7 x 4 = 28 instead of 7 + 7 + 7 + 7 = 28.

Directions: Multiply as fast as you can.

4 x7	7 x6	0 x8	
7 x2	9 x5	1 x5	6 x4
8 x3	7 x1	4 x2	9 x6
8 x5	6 x7	9 x8	3 x5 7 x8
3 x9	5 x6	9 x9	7 x5 9 x4
3 x6	2 x8		8 x6 7 x7
0 x7			3 x3 5 x9

Name: _____

Multiplication: Tens, Hundreds, And Thousands

Multiplication is a short way to find the sum of adding the same number a certain amount of times, such as 7 x 4 = 28 instead of 7 + 7 + 7 + 7 = 28.

Directions: Study the examples.

Examples:

When multiplying a number by 10, the answer is the number with a zero. It is like counting by 10s.

10	10	10	10	10	10
x1	x2	x3	x4	x5	x6
10	20	30	40	50	60

When multiplying a number by 100, the answer is the number with two zeroes.
When multiplying a number by 1000, the answer is the number with three zeroes.

100	100	100	1000	1000	1000
x1	x2	x3	x1	x2	x3
100	200	300	1000	2000	3000

Such basic facts help us multiply.

4	400	8	800	7	700
x2	x2	x3	x3	x5	x5
8	800	24	2400	35	3,500

Directions: Multiply.

10	60	400	700	50
x3	x5	x5	x8	x7

80	4000	6000	300	700
x9	x2	x4	x9	x6

3 x 800 = _____   9 x 2000 = _____   7 x 90 = _____

Name: _____

Multiplication: One-Digit Number x Two-Digit Number

Multiplication is a short way to find the sum of adding the same number a certain amount of times, such as 7 x 4 = 28 instead of 7 + 7 + 7 + 7 = 28.

Directions: Study the example. Follow the steps to multiplying by regrouping tens.

Example:

Step 1. Multiply ones. Regroup.

$$\begin{array}{r} {}^{2}54 \\ \underline{\times 7} \\ 8 \end{array}$$

Step 2. Multiply Tens. Add 2 tens.

$$\begin{array}{r} {}^{2}54 \\ \underline{\times 7} \\ 378 \end{array}$$

27	63	52	91	45
x3	x4	x5	x9	x7

75	64	76	93	87
x2	x5	x3	x6	x4

66	38	47	64	51
x7	x2	x8	x9	x8

99	13	32	25	15
x3	x7	x4	x8	x7

The chickens on the Smith farm produce 48 dozen eggs each day. How many dozen eggs do they produce in 7 days? _____

Name: _____

Multiplication: Two-Digit Number x Two-Digit Number

Multiplication is a short way to find the sum of adding the same number a certain amount of times, such as 7 x 4 = 28 instead of 7 + 7 + 7 + 7 = 28.

Directions: Study the examples. Follow the steps to multiply by regrouping.

Example:

Step 1. Multiply by ones. Regroup.   Step 2. Multiply by tens. Regroup. Add.

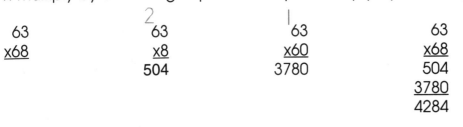

```
              2                    |
  63          63           63           63
 x68          x8          x60          x68
             504          3780          504
                                       3780
                                       4284
```

```
  12          27           65           19
 x55         x15          x27          x39
```

```
  99          35           43           38
 x13         x14          x26          x17
```

```
  53          47           57           48
 x86         x72          x62          x33
```

```
  27          93           64           53
 x54         x45          x16          x23
```

The Jones farm has 24 cows that each produce 52 quarts of milk a day.
How many quarts are produced each day altogether?   _____

Name: _____

Multiplication: Two-Digit Number x Three-Digit Number

Multiplication is a short way to find the sum of adding the same number a certain amount of times, such as 7 x 4 = 28 instead of 7 + 7 + 7 + 7 = 28.

Directions: Study the example. Follow the steps to multiply.

Example:

Step 1. Multiply by ones. Regroup.

```
                2 2
  287          287
  x43           x3
               861
```

Step 2. Multiply by tens. Regroup. Add.

```
   287          287
   x40          x43
 11,480         861
             11,480
             12,341
```

```
  261      434      357      614      368
  x36      x48      x75      x59      x98
```

```
  231      754      549      372      458
  x46      x65      x89      x94      x85
```

At the Douglas berry farm, workers pick 378 baskets of strawberries each day. Each basket holds 65 strawberries. How many strawberries are picked each day?

_____

Name: _____

Multiplication: Three-Digit Number x Three-Digit Number

Multiplication is a short way to find the sum of adding the same number a certain amount of times, such as 7 x 4 = 28 instead of 7 + 7 + 7 + 7 = 28.

Directions: Multiply. Regroup when needed.

Example:

```
      563
     x248
     4504
    22520
   112600
   139,624
```

Hint: When multiplying by the tens, start writing the number in the tens place. When multiplying by the hundreds, start in the hundreds place.

842 x167	932 x272	759 x468	531 x556
383 x476	523 x349	229 x189	738 x513
483 x148	946 x367	365 x622	

James grows pumpkins on his farm. He has 362 rows of pumpkins. There are 593 pumpkins in each row. How many pumpkins does James grow? _____

ANSWER KEY

This Answer Key has been designed so that it may be easily removed if you so desire.

MASTER MATH
4

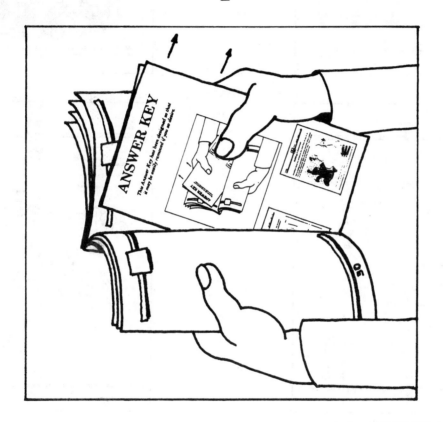

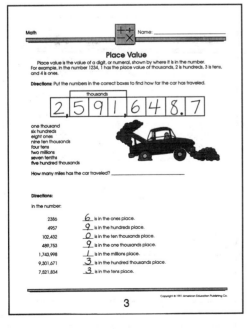

Math   Name: _____

Place Value

Place value is the value of a digit, or numeral, shown by where it is in the number. For example, in the number 1234, 1 has the place value of thousands, 2 is hundreds, 3 is tens, and 4 is ones.

Directions: Put the numbers in the correct boxes to find how far the car has traveled.

	thousands						
2,	5	9	1,	6	4	8.	7

one thousand
six hundreds
eight ones
nine ten thousands
four tens
two millions
seven tenths
five hundred thousands

How many miles has the car traveled? _____

Directions:

In the number:

2386	**6** is in the ones place.
4957	**9** is in the hundreds place.
102,432	**0** is in the ten thousands place.
489,753	**9** is in the one thousands place.
1,743,998	**1** is in the millions place.
9,301,671	**3** is in the hundred thousands place.
7,521,834	**3** is in the tens place.

3

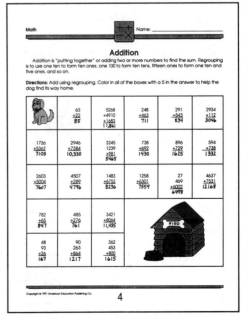

Math   Name: _____

Addition

Addition is "putting together" or adding two or more numbers to find the sum. Regrouping is to use one ten to form ten ones, one 100 to form ten tens, fifteen ones to form one ten and five ones, and so on.

Directions: Add using regrouping. Color in all of the boxes with a 5 in the answer to help the dog find its way home.

	63 +22 **85**	5268 +4910 +1683 **11,861**	248 +463 **711**	291 +543 **834**	2934 +112 **3046**
1736 +5367 **7103**	2946 +7384 **10,330**	3245 1239 +981 **5465**	738 +692 **1430**	896 +729 **1625**	594 +738 **1332**
2603 +5004 **7607**	4507 +289 **4796**	1483 +6753 **8236**	1258 +6301 **7559**	27 469 +6002 **6498**	4637 +7531 **12,168**
782 +65 **847**	485 +276 **761**	3421 +8064 **11,485**			
48 93 +26 **167**	90 263 +864 **1217**	362 453 +800 **1615**			

4

Subtraction

Subtraction is "taking away" or subtracting one number from another. Regrouping is to use one ten to form ten ones, one 100 to form ten tens, fifteen ones to form one ten and five ones, and so on.

Directions: Subtract using regrouping.

Examples:

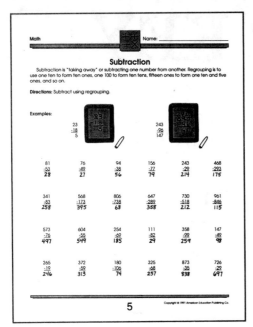

$$\begin{array}{r} 23 \\ -18 \\ \hline 5 \end{array} \qquad \begin{array}{r} 243 \\ -96 \\ \hline 147 \end{array}$$

81 -53 **28**	76 -49 **27**	94 -38 **56**	156 -77 **79**	243 -29 **214**	468 -293 **175**
341 -83 **258**	568 -173 **395**	806 -738 **68**	647 -289 **358**	730 -518 **212**	961 -846 **115**
573 -76 **497**	604 -55 **549**	254 -69 **185**	111 -82 **29**	358 -99 **259**	147 -49 **98**
265 -19 **246**	372 -59 **313**	180 -106 **74**	325 -68 **257**	873 -35 **838**	726 -29 **697**

Addition And Subtraction

Addition is "putting together" or adding two or more numbers to find the sum. Subtraction is "taking away" or subtracting one number from another.

Directions: Add or subtract.

38 43 +21 **102**	1269 2453 +8219 **11,941**	5792 -4814 **978**	629 491 +308 **1428**	4697 -2988 **1709**
5280 -3147 **2133**	68 27 +42 **137**	197 436 +213 **846**	7321 -2789 **4532**	456 +974 **1430**
3932 +6681 **8613**	492 863 +57 **1412**	9873 +5483 **15,356**	4978 +2131 **7109**	6235 +2986 **9221**

Sue stocked her pond with 263 bass and 187 trout. The turtles ate 97 fish. How many fish are left?   **353**

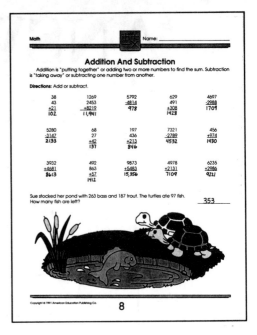

Rounding

Rounding a number means expressing it to the nearest ten, hundred, thousand, and so on.

Directions: Round the following numbers to the nearest ten. If the number has 5 ones or more, round it up to the next highest ten. For example, round 26 up to 30. If the number has 4 ones or less, round down to the nearest ten, such as rounding 44 down to 40.

18 **20**   33 **30**   82 **80**   56 **60**

24 **20**   49 **50**   91 **90**   67 **70**

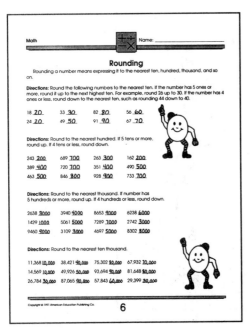

Directions: Round to the nearest hundred. If 5 tens or more, round up. If 4 tens or less, round down.

243 **200**   689 **700**   263 **300**   162 **200**

389 **400**   720 **700**   351 **400**   490 **500**

463 **500**   846 **800**   928 **900**   733 **700**

Directions: Round to the nearest thousand. If number has 5 hundreds or more, round up. If 4 hundreds or less, round down.

2638 **3000**   3940 **4000**   8653 **9000**   6238 **6000**

1429 **1000**   5061 **5000**   7289 **7000**   2742 **3000**

9460 **9000**   3109 **3000**   4697 **5000**   8302 **8000**

Directions: Round to the nearest ten thousand.

11,368 **10,000**   38,421 **40,000**   75,302 **80,000**   67,932 **70,000**

14,569 **10,000**   49,926 **50,000**   93,694 **90,000**   81,648 **80,000**

26,784 **30,000**   87,065 **90,000**   57,843 **60,000**   29,399 **30,000**

Multiples

A multiple is the product of a specific number and any other number. For example, the multiples of 2 are 2 (2 x 1) 4, (2 x 2), 6, 8, 10, 12, and so on.

Directions: Write the missing multiples.

Example: Count by fives.
5, 10, 15, 20, 25, 30, 35. These are multiples of 5.

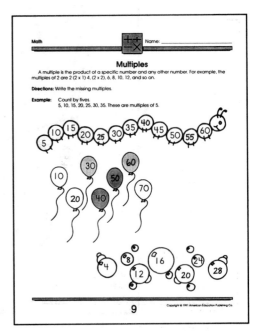

Addition And Subtraction

Addition is "putting together" or adding two or more numbers to find the sum. Subtraction is "taking away" or subtracting one number from another.

Regrouping is to use one ten to form ten ones, one 100 to form ten tens, fifteen ones to form one ten and five ones, and so on.

Directions: Add or subtract. Remember to regroup.

32 68 +43 **143**	183 246 +89 **518**	456 398 +597 **1451**	643 -377 **266**
1563 -941 **622**	3586 +4218 **7804**	8711 -4937 **3774**	9361 -7452 **1909**
			5734 +6298 **12,032**
293 431 +93 **817**	743 -529 **214**	849 250 +82 **1181**	1227 2431 +5792 **9450**
			9117 -3828 **5289**

68 + 93 + 146 = **307**   73 + 246 + 1579 = **1898**

43 + 745 - 29 = **759**   128 + 403 + 2571 = **3102**

156 + 627 + 541 = **1324**   97 + 51 + 37 + 79 = **264**

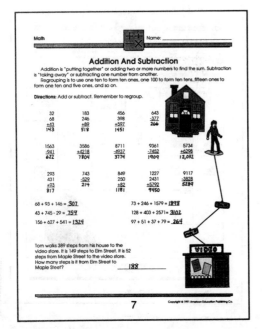

Tom walks 389 steps from his house to the video store. It is 149 steps from Maple Street to the video store. How many steps is it from Elm Street to Maple Street?   **188**

Review

Directions: Add or subtract using regrouping.

67 93 +48 **208**	5029 -3068 **1961**	732 801 +18 **1551**	2467 +3184 **5651**	8453 -6087 **2366**
5792 -3889 **1903**	7489 +5938 **13,427**	463 -209 **254**	3537 -2394 **1143**	6342 +959 **7301**

Directions: Write the numbers in the boxes.

		thousands					
8	,	4	0	0	,	9	5	2

eight million, four hundred thousand, nine hundred fifty two

		thousands					
5	3	5	,	0	4	1	.	2

five hundred thousands, three ten thousands, five thousands, zero hundreds, four tens, one one, two tenths

Directions: Fill in the blanks with the missing multiples.

6, 12, 18, **24** , 30, **36**   3, **6** , **9** , 12, 15

4, **8** , 12, 16, **20** , 24   **5** , 10, 15, **20** , **25**

Multiplication

Multiplication is a short way to find the sum of adding the same number a certain amount of times, such as 7 x 4 = 28 instead of 7 + 7 + 7 + 7 = 28.

Directions: Multiply as fast as you can.

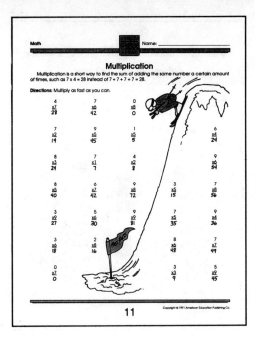

4 x7 **28**	7 x6 **42**	0 x8 **0**
7 x2 **14**	9 x5 **45**	1 x5 **5**
8 x3 **24**	7 x1 **7**	4 x2 **8**
8 x5 **40**	6 x7 **42**	9 x8 **72**
3 x9 **27**	5 x6 **30**	9 x9 **81**
3 x6 **18**	2 x8 **16**	
0 x7 **0**		

6
x4
24

9
x6
54

7
x8
56

7
x5
35

9
x4
36

8
x6
48

7
x7
49

3
x3
9

5
x9
45

Multiplication: Tens, Hundreds, And Thousands

Multiplication is a short way to find the sum of adding the same number a certain amount of times, such as 7 x 4 = 28 instead of 7 + 7 + 7 + 7 = 28.

Directions: Study the examples.

Examples:
When multiplying a number by 10, the answer is the number with a zero.
It is like counting by 10s.

10 x1 10	10 x2 20	10 x3 30	10 x4 40	10 x5 50	10 x6 60

When multiplying a number by 100, the answer is the number with two zeroes.
When multiplying a number by 1000, the answer is the number with three zeroes.

100 x1 100	100 x2 200	100 x3 300	1000 x1 1000	1000 x2 2000	1000 x3 3000

Such basic facts help us multiply.

4 x2 8	400 x2 800	8 x3 24	800 x3 2400	7 x5 35	700 x5 3,500

Directions: Multiply.

10 x3 **30**	60 x5 **300**	400 x5 **2000**	700 x8 **5600**	50 x7 **350**
80 x9 **720**	4000 x2 **8000**	6000 x4 **24,000**	300 x9 **2700**	700 x6 **4200**

3 x 800 = **2400**   9 x 2000 = **18,000**   7 x 90 = **630**

Multiplication: One-Digit Number x Two-Digit Number

Multiplication is a short way to find the sum of adding the same number a certain amount of times, such as 7 x 4 = 28 instead of 7 + 7 + 7 + 7 = 28.

Directions: Study the example. Follow the steps to multiplying by regrouping tens.

Example:

Step 1. Multiply ones. Regroup.

2
54
x7
8

Step 2. Multiply Tens. Add 2 tens.

2
54
x7
378

27 x3 **81**	63 x4 **252**	52 x5 **260**	91 x9 **819**	45 x7 **315**
75 x2 **150**	64 x5 **320**	76 x3 **228**	93 x6 **558**	87 x4 **348**
66 x7 **462**	38 x2 **76**	47 x8 **376**	64 x9 **576**	51 x8 **408**
99 x3 **297**	13 x7 **91**	32 x4 **128**	25 x8 **200**	15 x7 **105**

The chickens on the Smith farm produce 48 dozen eggs each day. How many dozen eggs do they produce in 7 days?   **336**

Multiplication: Two-Digit Number x Two-Digit Number

Multiplication is a short way to find the sum of adding the same number a certain amount of times, such as 7 x 4 = 28 instead of 7 + 7 + 7 + 7 = 28.

Directions: Study the examples. Follow the steps to multiply by regrouping.

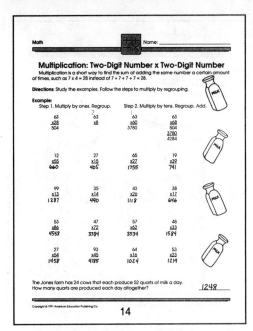

Example:

Step 1. Multiply by ones. Regroup.

63
x28
504

2
63
x8

Step 2. Multiply by tens. Regroup. Add.

63
x60
3780

63
x68
504
3780
4284

12 x55 **660**	27 x15 **405**	65 x27 **1755**	19 x39 **741**
99 x13 **1287**	35 x14 **490**	43 x26 **1118**	38 x17 **646**
53 x86 **4558**	47 x72 **3384**	57 x62 **3534**	48 x33 **1584**
27 x54 **1458**	93 x45 **4185**	64 x16 **1024**	53 x23 **1219**

The Jones farm has 24 cows that each produce 52 quarts of milk a day. How many quarts are produced each day altogether?   **1248**

Multiplication: Two-Digit Number x Three-Digit Number

Multiplication is a short way to find the sum of adding the same number a certain amount of times, such as 7 x 4 = 28 instead of 7 + 7 + 7 + 7 = 28.

Directions: Study the example. Follow the steps to multiply.

Example:

Step 1. Multiply by ones. Regroup.

287
x43
861

287
x3
861

Step 2. Multiply by tens. Regroup. Add.

287
x40
11,480

287
x43
861
11,480
12,341

261 x36 **9,396**	434 x48 **20,832**	357 x75 **26,775**	614 x59 **36,226**	368 x98 **36,064**
231 x46 **10,626**	754 x65 **49,010**	549 x89 **48,861**	372 x94 **34,968**	458 x85 **38,930**

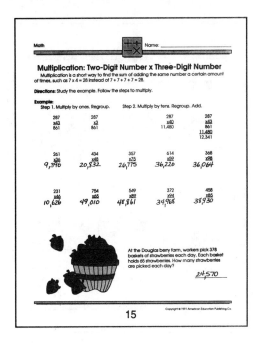

At the Douglas berry farm, workers pick 378 baskets of strawberries each day. Each basket holds 65 strawberries. How many strawberries are picked each day?   **24,570**

Multiplication: Three-Digit Number x Three-Digit Number

Multiplication is a short way to find the sum of adding the same number a certain amount of times, such as 7 x 4 = 28 instead of 7 + 7 + 7 + 7 = 28.

Directions: Multiply. Regroup when needed.

Example:

563
x248
4504
2252
1126
139,624

Hint: When multiplying by the tens, start writing the number in the tens place. When multiplying by the hundreds, start in the hundreds place.

842 x167 **140,614**	932 x272 **253,604**	759 x468 **355,212**	531 x556 **295,236**
383 x476 **182,308**	523 x349 **182,527**	229 x189 **43,281**	738 x513 **378,594**
483 x148 **71,484**	946 x367 **347,182**	365 x622 **227,030**	

James grows pumpkins on his farm. He has 362 rows of pumpkins. There are 593 pumpkins in each row. How many pumpkins does James grow?   **214,666**

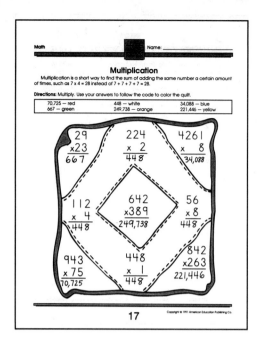

Multiplication

Multiplication is a short way to find the sum of adding the same number a certain amount of times, such as 7 x 4 = 28 instead of 7 + 7 + 7 + 7 = 28.

Directions: Multiply. Use your answers to follow the code to color the quilt.

70,725 — red	448 — white	34,088 — blue
667 — green	249,738 — orange	221,446 — yellow

$$\begin{array}{r}29\\ \times 23\\\hline 667\end{array}\quad\begin{array}{r}224\\ \times 2\\\hline 448\end{array}\quad\begin{array}{r}4261\\ \times 8\\\hline 34,088\end{array}$$

$$\begin{array}{r}112\\ \times 4\\\hline 448\end{array}\quad\begin{array}{r}642\\ \times 389\\\hline 249,738\end{array}\quad\begin{array}{r}56\\ \times 8\\\hline 448\end{array}$$

$$\begin{array}{r}943\\ \times 75\\\hline 70,725\end{array}\quad\begin{array}{r}448\\ \times 1\\\hline 448\end{array}\quad\begin{array}{r}842\\ \times 263\\\hline 221,446\end{array}$$

Copyright © 1991 American Education Publishing Co.

17

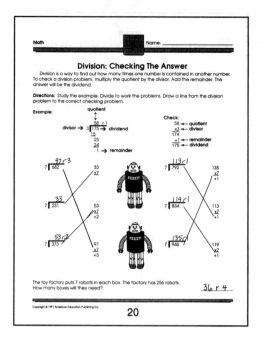

Division: Checking The Answer

Division is a way to find out how many times one number is contained in another number. To check a division problem, multiply the quotient by the divisor. Add the remainder. The answer will be the dividend.

Directions: Study the example. Divide to work the problems. Draw a line from the division problem to the correct checking problem.

Example:

$$\text{divisor}\to 3\overline{)175}\gets\text{dividend}$$

Check:
$$\begin{array}{r}58\gets\text{quotient}\\ \times 3\gets\text{divisor}\\\hline 174\\ +1\gets\text{remainder}\\\hline 175\gets\text{dividend}\end{array}$$

$7\overline{)682}\;97\,r3$　　33 ×7

$7\overline{)231}\;33$　　53 ×7 +2

$7\overline{)373}\;53\,r2$　　97 ×7 +3

$7\overline{)792}\;113\,r1$　　135 ×1 +1

$7\overline{)834}\;119\,r1$　　113 ×7 +1

$7\overline{)946}\;135\,r1$　　119 ×7 +1

The toy factory puts 7 robots in each box. The factory has 256 robots. How many boxes will they need?　　36 r 4

Copyright © 1991 American Education Publishing Co.

20

Review

Directions: Multiply. Work the problem in the box. Color the ribbons blue if the answer is correct.

$$\begin{array}{r}5683\\ \times 9\\\hline 51,147\end{array}\quad\begin{array}{r}256\\ \times 38\\\hline 2048\\ 768\\\hline 9728\end{array}\quad\begin{array}{r}489\\ \times 56\\\hline 2934\\ 2445\\\hline 27384\end{array}$$

$$\begin{array}{r}356\\ \times 427\\\hline 2492\\ 712\\ 1424\\\hline 152,012\end{array}\quad\begin{array}{r}800\\ \times 7\\\hline 5600\end{array}\quad\begin{array}{r}60\\ \times 5\\\hline 300\end{array}$$

Copyright © 1991 American Education Publishing Co.

18

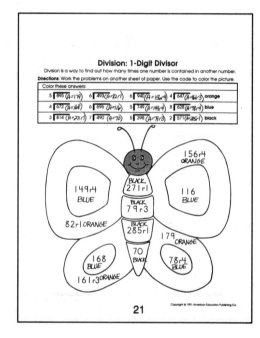

Division: 1-Digit Divisor

Division is a way to find out how many times one number is contained in another number.

Directions: Work the problems on another sheet of paper. Use the code to color the picture.

Color these answers:

5$\overline{)895}$ (A=179)	6$\overline{)493}$ (A=82r1)	6$\overline{)940}$ (A=156r4)	5$\overline{)547}$ (A=109r3)	orange
4$\overline{)672}$ (A=168)	6$\overline{)695}$ (A=116r)	5$\overline{)745}$ (A=149r4)	8$\overline{)628}$ (A=78r4)	blue
3$\overline{)814}$ (A=271r1)	7$\overline{)490}$ (A=70)	5$\overline{)398}$ (A=79r3)	2$\overline{)571}$ (A=285r1)	black

156 r 4 ORANGE

BLACK 271 r 1

149 r 4 BLUE

116 BLUE

BLACK 79 r 3

82 r 1 ORANGE

BLACK 285 r 1

179 ORANGE

168 BLUE

70 BLACK

78 r 4 BLUE

161 r 3 ORANGE

Copyright © 1991 American Education Publishing Co.

21

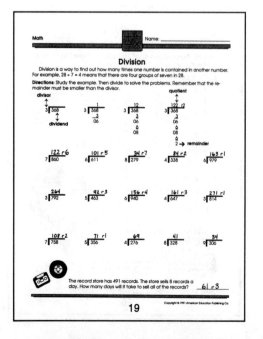

Division

Division is a way to find out how many times one number is contained in another number. For example, 28 ÷ 7 = 4 means that there are four groups of seven in 28.

Directions: Study the example. Then divide to solve the problems. Remember that the remainder must be smaller than the divisor.

$$\text{divisor}\;3\overline{)308}\gets\text{dividend}$$

quotient $\to 3\overline{)308}$ remainder → 2

$7\overline{)860}\;122\,r6$　$6\overline{)611}\;101\,r5$　$8\overline{)279}\;34\,r7$　$4\overline{)338}\;84\,r2$　$6\overline{)979}\;163\,r1$

$3\overline{)792}\;264$　$5\overline{)463}\;92\,r3$　$6\overline{)940}\;156\,r4$　$4\overline{)647}\;161\,r3$　$3\overline{)814}\;271\,r1$

$7\overline{)758}\;108\,r2$　$5\overline{)356}\;71\,r1$　$4\overline{)276}\;69$　$8\overline{)328}\;41$　$9\overline{)306}\;34$

The record store has 491 records. The store sells 8 records a day. How many days will it take to sell all of the records?　　61 r 3

Copyright © 1991 American Education Publishing Co.

19

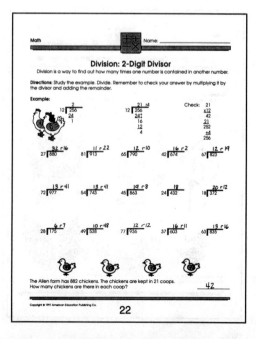

Division: 2-Digit Divisor

Division is a way to find out how many times one number is contained in another number.

Directions: Study the example. Divide. Remember to check your answer by multiplying it by the divisor and adding the remainder.

Example:

$$12\overline{)256}\;21\,r4$$
$$\begin{array}{r}24\\\hline 16\\ 12\\\hline 4\end{array}$$

Check:
$$\begin{array}{r}21\\ \times 12\\\hline 42\\ 21\\\hline 252\\ +4\\\hline 256\end{array}$$

$27\overline{)880}\;32\,r16$　$81\overline{)913}\;11\,r22$　$65\overline{)790}\;12\,r10$　$42\overline{)674}\;16\,r2$　$67\overline{)823}\;12\,r19$

$72\overline{)977}\;13\,r41$　$54\overline{)743}\;13\,r41$　$45\overline{)863}\;19\,r8$　$24\overline{)432}\;18$　$18\overline{)372}\;20\,r12$

$28\overline{)175}\;6\,r7$　$49\overline{)538}\;10\,r48$　$77\overline{)936}\;12\,r12$　$37\overline{)603}\;16\,r11$　$63\overline{)835}\;13\,r16$

The Allen farm has 882 chickens. The chickens are kept in 21 coops. How many chickens are there in each coop?　　42

Copyright © 1991 American Education Publishing Co.

22

Division: Checking The Answer

Division is a way to find out how many times one number is contained in another number.

Directions: Divide, then check your answers.

Example:

```
      182 r1        Check:    182
  4 729                        x4
    4                         728
    32                        + 1
    32                        729
     9
     8
     1
```

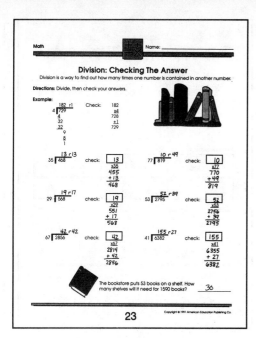

```
      13 r13     check:  13
 35 468                 x35
                        455
                       + 13
                        468

      10 r 49    check:  10
 77 819                 x77
                        770
                       + 49
                        819

      19 r17     check:  19
 29 568                 x29
                        551
                       + 17
                        568

      52 r39     check:  52
 53 2795                x53
                       2756
                       + 39
                       2795

      42 r42     check:  42
 67 2856                x67
                       2814
                       + 42
                       2856

      155 r27    check:  155
 41 6382                x41
                       6355
                       + 27
                       6382
```

The bookstore puts 53 books on a shelf. How many shelves will it need for 1590 books?   **30**

Review

Directions: Divide.

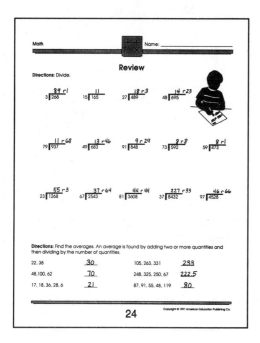

```
      89 r1          11            18 r3         14 r23
 3 268         15 165         27 489         48 695

      11 r68        13 r46        9 r29         8 r8          8 r1
 79 937        49 683        91 848        73 592        59 473

      55 r3         37 r64        44 r44        227 r33       46 r66
 23 1268       67 2543       81 3608       37 8432       97 4528
```

Directions: Find the averages. An average is found by adding two or more quantities and then dividing by the number of quantities.

22, 38	**30**	105, 263, 331	**233**
48, 100, 62	**70**	248, 325, 250, 67	**222.5**
17, 18, 36, 28, 6	**21**	87, 91, 55, 48, 119	**80**

Fraction: Addition

A fraction is a number that names part of a whole, such as 1/2 or 1/3. The denominator is the bottom number in a fraction; the numerator is the top number.
When adding fractions with the same denominator, the denominator stays the same. Add only the numerators.

Example:

numerator → $\frac{1}{8}$ + $\frac{2}{8}$ = $\frac{3}{8}$ ← denominator

Directions: Study the example. Add the fractions. The first one is done for you.

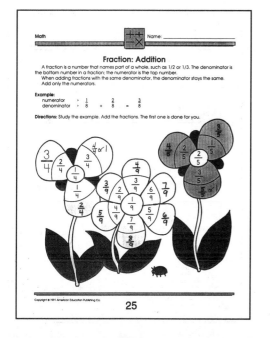

Fractions: Subtraction

A fraction is a number that names part of a whole, such as 1/2 or 1/3. The denominator is the bottom number in a fraction; the numerator is the top number.
When subtracting fractions with the same denominator, the denominator stays the same. Subtract only the numerators.

Directions: Solve the problems below, working from left to right across each row. As you find each answer, copy the letter from the code box into the numbered blanks. The first one is done for you. The answer will tell the name of a famous American.

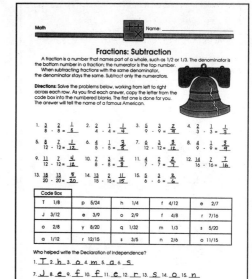

1. $\frac{3}{8} - \frac{2}{8} = \frac{1}{8}$
2. $\frac{2}{4} - \frac{1}{4} = \frac{1}{4}$
3. $\frac{5}{9} - \frac{3}{9} = \frac{2}{9}$
4. $\frac{2}{3} - \frac{1}{3} = \frac{1}{3}$

5. $\frac{8}{12} - \frac{7}{12} = \frac{1}{12}$
6. $\frac{4}{5} - \frac{1}{5} = \frac{3}{5}$
7. $\frac{5}{12} - \frac{2}{12} = \frac{3}{12}$
8. $\frac{4}{7} - \frac{1}{7} = \frac{3}{7}$

9. $\frac{11}{12} - \frac{7}{12} = \frac{4}{12}$
10. $\frac{7}{8} - \frac{3}{8} = \frac{4}{8}$
11. $\frac{4}{7} - \frac{2}{7} = \frac{2}{7}$
12. $\frac{14}{16} - \frac{7}{16} = \frac{7}{16}$

13. $\frac{18}{20} - \frac{13}{20} = \frac{5}{20}$
14. $\frac{13}{15} - \frac{11}{15} = \frac{2}{15}$
15. $\frac{5}{6} - \frac{2}{6} = \frac{3}{6}$

Code Box							
T	1/8	p	5/24	h	1/4	f	4/12	e	2/7
J	3/12	e	3/9	o	2/9	f	4/8	r	7/16
o	2/8	y	8/20	q	1/32	m	1/3	s	5/20
a	1/12	r	12/15	s	3/5	n	2/6	o	11/15

Who helped write the Declaration of independence?

1. **T** 2. **h** 3. **e** 4. **o** 5. **m** 6. **a** 7. **s**

7. **J** 8. **e** 9. **f** 10. **f** 11. **e** 12. **r** 13. **s** 14. **o** 15. **n**

Fractions: Adding Mixed Numerals

A mixed numeral is a number written as a whole number and a fraction, such as 6 5/8.

Directions: Add the number in the center to the numbers in the rings.

Example:

```
   9  1/3          2  3/6
  +3  1/3         +1  1/6
  12  2/3          3  4/6
```

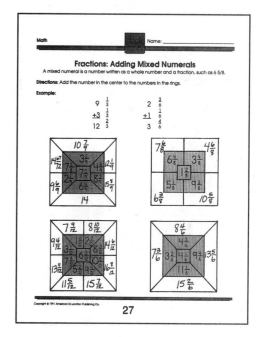

Fractions: Subtracting Mixed Numerals

A mixed numeral is a number written as a whole number and a fraction, such as 6 5/8.

Directions: Solve the problems. The first one is done for you.

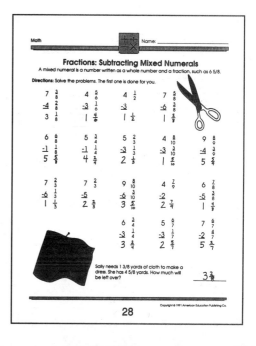

```
  7  3/8       4  5/6       4  4/6       7  5/8
 -4  2/8      -3  1/6      -3         -6  1/8
  3  1/8       1  4/6       1  1/2      1  4/8

  6  8/9       5  3/4       5  2/3       4  8/10      9
 -1  1/9      -1  1/4      -3  1/3      -3  2/10     -4  3/4
  5  7/9       4            2  1/3       1            5  1/4

  7  2/3       7  2/4       9  8/10      4  7/9       6  2/8
 -6  1/3      -5           -6  3/10     -2  1/9      -1  4/8
  1  1/3       2  2/4       3  5/10      2  7/9       5  4/8

               6  3/4       5  4/9       7  5/7
              -3  1/4      -3  1/9      -2  4/7
               3  2/4       2  3/9       5  1/7
```

Sally needs 1 3/8 yards of cloth to make a dress. She has 4 5/8 yards. How much will be left over?   **3 2/8**

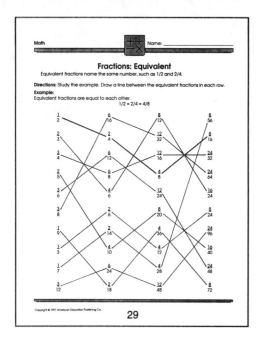

Math   Name: _____

Fractions: Equivalent

Equivalent fractions name the same number, such as 1/2 and 2/4.

Directions: Study the example. Draw a line between the equivalent fractions in each row.

Example:
Equivalent fractions are equal to each other.
$$1/2 = 2/4 = 4/8$$

$\frac{1}{2}$	$\frac{8}{16}$, $\frac{12}{8}$	$\frac{8}{56}$
$\frac{2}{3}$	$\frac{2}{4}$	$\frac{12}{32}$, $\frac{8}{16}$
$\frac{3}{4}$	$\frac{6}{12}$	$\frac{12}{8}$, $\frac{24}{32}$
$\frac{2}{5}$	$\frac{4}{8}$	$\frac{24}{64}$
$\frac{3}{6}$	$\frac{12}{24}$	$\frac{16}{24}$
$\frac{3}{4}$	$\frac{2}{8}$	$\frac{8}{24}$
$\frac{1}{9}$	$\frac{20}{8}$	$\frac{24}{96}$
$\frac{2}{14}$	$\frac{4}{36}$	$\frac{16}{40}$
$\frac{1}{3}$	$\frac{4}{10}$	$\frac{4}{12}$
$\frac{1}{7}$	$\frac{6}{24}$	$\frac{4}{28}$, $\frac{24}{48}$
$\frac{3}{12}$	$\frac{2}{18}$	$\frac{12}{48}$, $\frac{8}{72}$

Copyright © 1991 American Education Publishing Co.

29

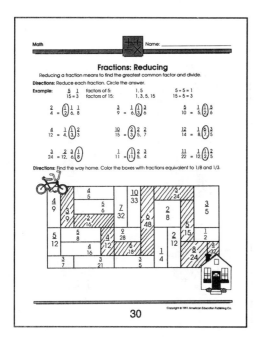

Math   Name: _____

Fractions: Reducing

Reducing a fraction means to find the greatest common factor and divide.

Directions: Reduce each fraction. Circle the answer.

Example: $\frac{5}{15} = \frac{1}{3}$ factors of 5: 1, 5   5 ÷ 5 = 1   factors of 15: 1, 3, 5, 15   15 ÷ 5 = 3

$\frac{2}{4} = $ ⓵ $\frac{1}{2}$ $\frac{1}{6}$, 8 $\frac{3}{9} = \frac{1}{6}$ ③ $\frac{3}{6}$ $\frac{5}{10} = \frac{5}{2}$ ⑤ $\frac{5}{6}$

$\frac{4}{12} = \frac{1}{4}$ ③ $\frac{2}{3}$ $\frac{10}{15} = $ ② $\frac{3}{5}$, 7 $\frac{12}{14} = \frac{1}{8}$ ⑥ $\frac{4}{5}$

$\frac{3}{24} = \frac{2}{12}$ $\frac{3}{4}$ ⑧ $\frac{1}{11} = $ ① $\frac{1}{11}$ $\frac{2}{5}$, 4 $\frac{11}{22} = \frac{1}{2}$ ① $\frac{2}{2}$

Directions: Find the way home. Color the boxes with fractions equivalent to 1/8 and 1/3.

30

Copyright © 1991 American Education Publishing Co.

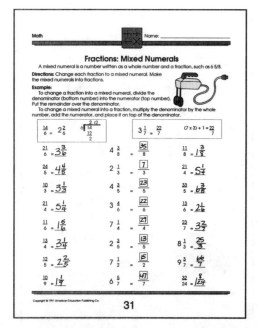

Math   Name: _____

Fractions: Mixed Numerals

A mixed numeral is a number written as a whole number and a fraction, such as 6 5/8.

Directions: Change each fraction to a mixed numeral. Make the mixed numerals into fractions.

Example:
To change a fraction into a mixed numeral, divide the denominator (bottom number) into the numerator (top number). Put the remainder over the denominator.
To change a mixed numeral into a fraction, multiply the denominator by the whole number, add the numerator, and place it on top of the denominator.

$\frac{14}{6} = 2\frac{2}{6}$ $3\frac{1}{7} = \frac{22}{7}$ (7 × 3) + 1 = $\frac{22}{7}$

$\frac{21}{6} = 3\frac{3}{6}$ $4\frac{3}{8} = \frac{35}{8}$ $\frac{11}{8} = 1\frac{3}{8}$

$\frac{24}{5} = 4\frac{4}{5}$ $2\frac{1}{3} = \frac{7}{3}$ $\frac{21}{4} = 5\frac{1}{4}$

$\frac{10}{3} = 3\frac{1}{3}$ $4\frac{3}{5} = \frac{23}{5}$ $\frac{33}{5} = 6\frac{3}{5}$

$\frac{21}{4} = 5\frac{1}{4}$ $3\frac{4}{6} = \frac{22}{6}$ $\frac{13}{6} = 2\frac{1}{6}$

$\frac{11}{6} = 1\frac{5}{6}$ $7\frac{1}{4} = \frac{29}{4}$ $\frac{23}{7} = 3\frac{2}{7}$

$\frac{13}{4} = 3\frac{1}{4}$ $2\frac{3}{5} = \frac{13}{5}$ $8\frac{1}{3} = \frac{25}{3}$

$\frac{12}{5} = 2\frac{2}{5}$ $7\frac{1}{2} = \frac{15}{2}$ $9\frac{3}{7} = \frac{66}{7}$

$\frac{10}{9} = 1\frac{1}{9}$ $6\frac{5}{7} = \frac{47}{7}$ $\frac{32}{24} = 1\frac{8}{24}$

Copyright © 1991 American Education Publishing Co.

31

Math   Name: _____

Review

Directions: Add or subtract the fractions and mixed numerals.

$\frac{3}{8} - \frac{1}{8} = \frac{2}{8}$ $\frac{3}{4} - \frac{2}{4} = \frac{1}{4}$ $\frac{3}{5} + \frac{1}{5} = \frac{4}{5}$ $\frac{4}{12} + \frac{3}{12} = \frac{7}{12}$ $\frac{3}{9} + \frac{1}{9} = \frac{4}{9}$

$3\frac{1}{8}$ $4\frac{5}{6}$ $7\frac{5}{6}$ $8\frac{3}{9}$ $4\frac{7}{8}$
$+1\frac{3}{8}$ $-3\frac{1}{6}$ $+3\frac{5}{11}$ $+2\frac{5}{9}$ $-2\frac{5}{8}$
$4\frac{4}{8}$ $1\frac{4}{6}$ $10\frac{8}{11}$ $10\frac{8}{9}$ $2\frac{2}{8}$

Directions: Reduce the fractions. Circle the answers.

$\frac{3}{6} = \frac{1}{7}$ ⑫ $\frac{1}{4}$	$\frac{2}{8} = \frac{1}{3}$ ⑭ $\frac{1}{16}$	$\frac{4}{6} = \frac{1}{4}$ ⑳ $\frac{3}{9}$
$\frac{4}{20} = \frac{1}{3}$ ⑮	$\frac{7}{21} = \frac{1}{7}$ ⑬ $\frac{1}{5}$	$\frac{9}{12} = \frac{3}{5}$ $\frac{1}{8}$ ⑳

Directions: Reduce the fractions.

$\frac{6}{24} = \frac{1}{4}$ $\frac{8}{32} = \frac{1}{4}$ $\frac{2}{4} = \frac{1}{2}$

$\frac{3}{15} = \frac{1}{5}$ $\frac{6}{12} = \frac{1}{6}$ $\frac{3}{9} = \frac{1}{3}$

Directions: Change the mixed numerals to fractions and the fractions to mixed numerals.

$3\frac{1}{3} = \frac{10}{3}$ $\frac{14}{4} = 3\frac{1}{2}$ $\frac{26}{6} = 4\frac{1}{3}$ $3\frac{7}{12} = \frac{43}{12}$ $\frac{22}{7} = 3\frac{1}{7}$

Copyright © 1991 American Education Publishing Co.

32

NOTES

Name: _____

Multiplication

Multiplication is a short way to find the sum of adding the same number a certain amount of times, such as 7 x 4 = 28 instead of 7 + 7 + 7 + 7 = 28.

Directions: Multiply. Use your answers to follow the code to color the quilt.

70,725 — red	448 — white	34,088 — blue
667 — green	249,738 — orange	221,446 — yellow

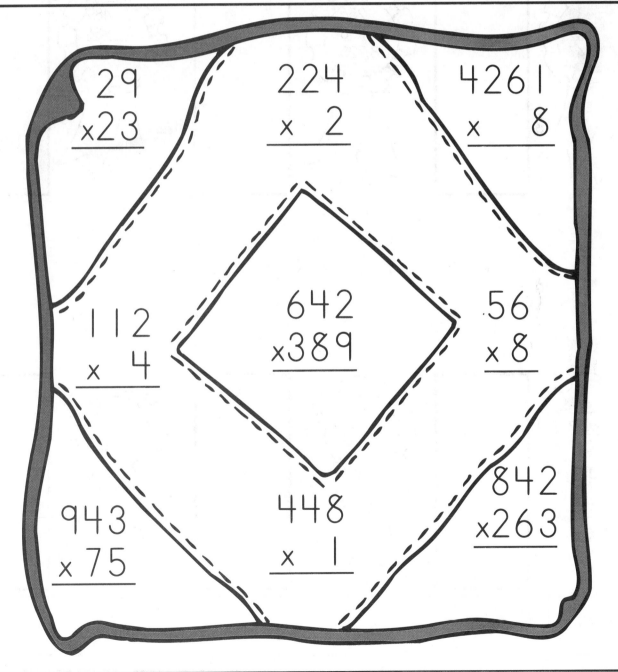

Name: _____

Review

Directions: Multiply. Work the problem in the box. Color the ribbons blue if the answer is correct.

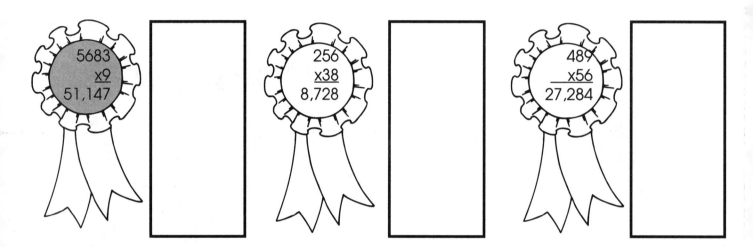

5683
x9
51,147

256
x38
8,728

489
x56
27,284

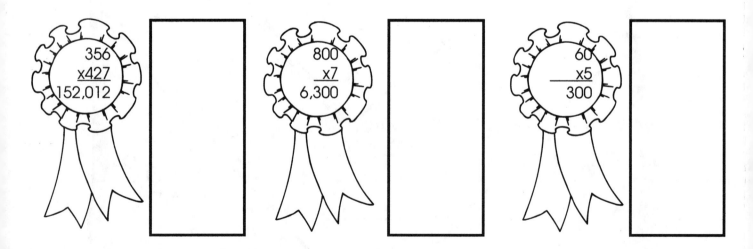

356
x427
152,012

800
x7
6,300

60
x5
300

Name: _____

Division

Division is a way to find out how many times one number is contained in another number. For example, 28 ÷ 7 = 4 means that there are four groups of seven in 28.

Directions: Study the example. Then divide to solve the problems. Remember that the remainder must be smaller than the divisor.

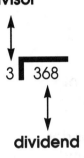

divisor

$3\overline{)368}$

dividend

```
      1
3 ) 368
    3
    06
```

```
     12
3 ) 368
    3
    06
    6
    08
```

quotient

```
    122 r2
3 ) 368
    3
    06
    6
    08
    6
    2  → remainder
```

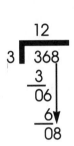

$7\overline{)860}$ $6\overline{)611}$ $8\overline{)279}$ $4\overline{)338}$ $6\overline{)979}$

$3\overline{)792}$ $5\overline{)463}$ $6\overline{)940}$ $4\overline{)647}$ $3\overline{)814}$

$7\overline{)758}$ $5\overline{)356}$ $4\overline{)276}$ $8\overline{)328}$ $9\overline{)306}$

The record store has 491 records. The store sells 8 records a day. How many days will it take to sell all of the records? _____

Division: Checking The Answer

Division is a way to find out how many times one number is contained in another number. To check a division problem, multiply the quotient by the divisor. Add the remainder. The answer will be the dividend.

Directions: Study the example. Divide to work the problems. Draw a line from the division problem to the correct checking problem.

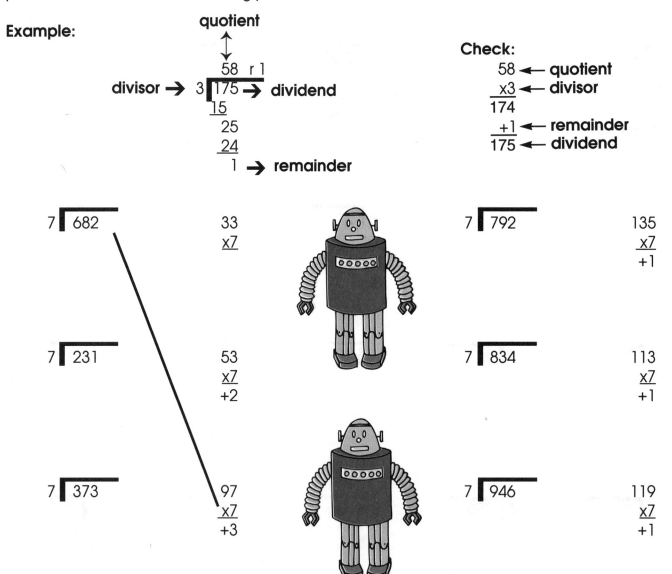

Example:

quotient

58 r 1

divisor → 3⟌175 → dividend
15
25
24
1 → remainder

Check:

58 ← quotient
x3 ← divisor
174
+1 ← remainder
175 ← dividend

7⟌682   33
                x7

7⟌792   135
                x7
                +1

7⟌231   53
                x7
                +2

7⟌834   113
                x7
                +1

7⟌373   97
                x7
                +3

7⟌946   119
                x7
                +1

The toy factory puts 7 robots in each box. The factory has 256 robots. How many boxes will they need? _____

Division: 1-Digit Divisor

Division is a way to find out how many times one number is contained in another number.

Directions: Work the problems on another sheet of paper. Use the code to color the picture.

Color these answers:				
5⟌895	6⟌493	6⟌940	4⟌647	**orange**
4⟌672	6⟌696	5⟌749	8⟌628	**blue**
3⟌814	7⟌490	5⟌398	2⟌571	**black**

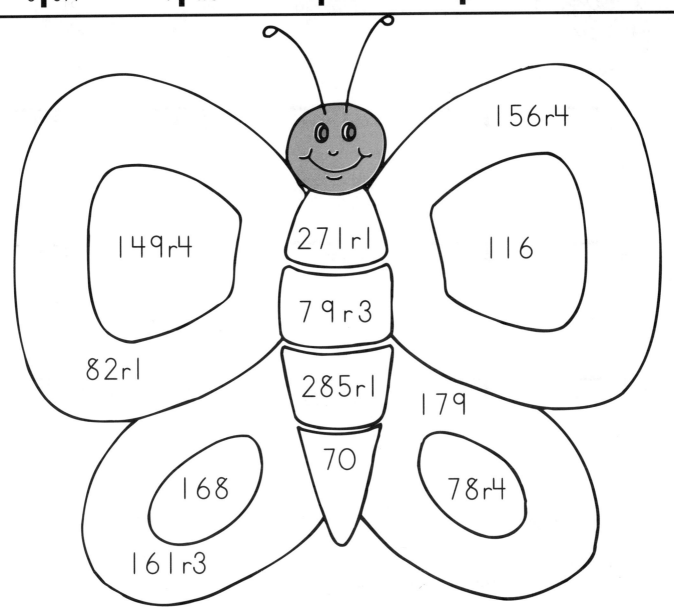

Name: _____

Division: 2-Digit Divisor

Division is a way to find out how many times one number is contained in another number.

Directions: Study the example. Divide. Remember to check your answer by multiplying it by the divisor and adding the remainder.

Example:

```
        2
12 | 256
    24
     1
```

```
     21  r4
12 | 256
    24↕
    16
    12
     4
```

Check: 21
        x12
         42
         21
        252
         +4
        256

```
27 | 880        81 | 913        65 | 790        42 | 674        67 | 823
```

```
72 | 977        54 | 743        45 | 863        24 | 432        18 | 372
```

```
28 | 175        49 | 538        77 | 936        37 | 603        63 | 835
```

The Allen farm has 882 chickens. The chickens are kept in 21 coops. How many chickens are there in each coop? _____

Name: _____

Division: Checking The Answer

Division is a way to find out how many times one number is contained in another number.

Directions: Divide, then check your answers.

Example:

```
    182  r1          Check:    182
4 | 729                         x4
    4                          728
    32                          +1
    32                         729
     9
     8
     1
```

```
35 | 468        check:    [     ]
                          x35
```

```
77 | 819        check:    [     ]
                          x77
```

```
29 | 568        check:    [     ]
                          x29
```

```
53 | 2795       check:    [     ]
                          x53
```

```
67 | 2856       check:    [     ]
                          x67
```

```
41 | 6382       check:    [     ]
                          x41
```

The bookstore puts 53 books on a shelf. How many shelves will it need for 1590 books? _____

Review

Directions: Divide.

3 ⟌ 268   15 ⟌ 165   27 ⟌ 489   48 ⟌ 695

79 ⟌ 937   49 ⟌ 683   91 ⟌ 848   73 ⟌ 592   59 ⟌ 473

23 ⟌ 1268   67 ⟌ 2543   81 ⟌ 3608   37 ⟌ 8432   97 ⟌ 4528

Directions: Find the averages. An average is found by adding two or more quantities and then dividing by the number of quantities.

22, 38 _____   105, 263, 331 _____

48, 100, 62 _____   248, 325, 250, 69 _____

17, 18, 36, 28, 6 _____   87, 91, 55, 48, 119 _____

Name: _____

Fraction: Addition

A fraction is a number that names part of a whole, such as 1/2 or 1/3. The denominator is the bottom number in a fraction; the numerator is the top number.

When adding fractions with the same denominator, the denominator stays the same. Add only the numerators.

Example:

numerator $\rightarrow$ $\dfrac{1}{8}$ $+$ $\dfrac{2}{8}$ $=$ $\dfrac{3}{8}$
denominator $\rightarrow$

Directions: Study the example. Add the fractions. The first one is done for you.

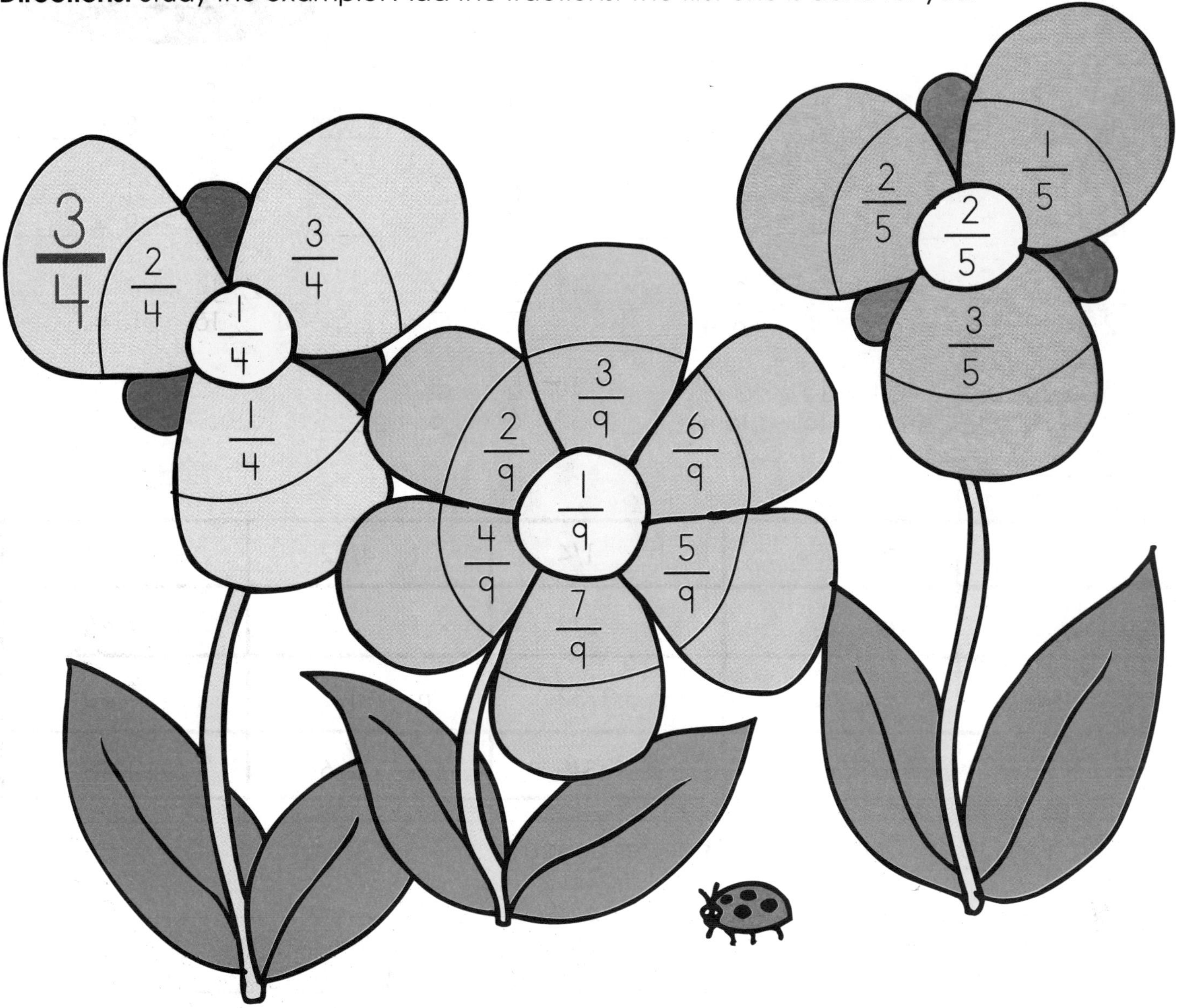

Name: _____

Fractions: Subtraction

A fraction is a number that names part of a whole, such as 1/2 or 1/3. The denominator is the bottom number in a fraction; the numerator is the top number.

When subtracting fractions with the same denominator, the denominator stays the same. Subtract only the numerators.

Directions: Solve the problems below, working from left to right across each row. As you find each answer, copy the letter from the code box into the numbered blanks. The first one is done for you. The answer will tell the name of a famous American.

1. $\frac{3}{8}$ - $\frac{2}{8}$ = $\frac{1}{8}$ 2. $\frac{2}{4}$ - $\frac{1}{4}$ = ____   3. $\frac{5}{9}$ - $\frac{3}{9}$ = ____   4. $\frac{2}{3}$ - $\frac{1}{3}$ = ____

5. $\frac{8}{12}$ - $\frac{7}{12}$ = ____   6. $\frac{4}{5}$ - $\frac{1}{5}$ = ____   7. $\frac{6}{12}$ - $\frac{3}{12}$ = ____   8. $\frac{4}{9}$ - $\frac{1}{9}$ = ____

9. $\frac{11}{12}$ - $\frac{7}{12}$ = ____   10. $\frac{7}{8}$ - $\frac{3}{8}$ = ____   11. $\frac{4}{7}$ - $\frac{2}{7}$ = ____   12. $\frac{14}{16}$ - $\frac{7}{16}$ = ____

13. $\frac{18}{20}$ - $\frac{13}{20}$ = ____   14. $\frac{13}{15}$ - $\frac{2}{15}$ = ____   15. $\frac{5}{6}$ - $\frac{3}{6}$ = ____

Code Box				
T 1/8	p 5/24	h 1/4	f 4/12	e 2/7
J 3/12	e 3/9	o 2/9	f 4/8	r 7/16
o 2/8	y 8/20	q 1/32	m 1/3	s 5/20
a 1/12	r 12/15	s 3/5	n 2/6	o 11/15

Who helped write the Declaration of Independence?

1. ____ 2. ____ 3. ____ 4. ____ 5. ____ 6. ____

7. ____ 8. ____ 9. ____ 10. ____ 11. ____ 12. ____ 13. ____ 14. ____ 15. ____

Name: _____

Fractions: Adding Mixed Numerals

A mixed numeral is a number written as a whole number and a fraction, such as 6 5/8.

Directions: Add the number in the center to the numbers in the rings.

Example:

$$9\frac{1}{3}$$
$$\underline{+3\frac{1}{3}}$$
$$12\frac{2}{3}$$

$$2\frac{3}{6}$$
$$\underline{+1\frac{1}{6}}$$
$$3\frac{4}{6}$$

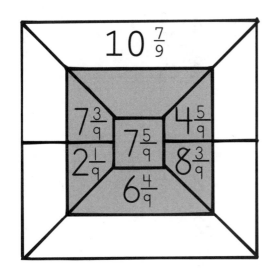

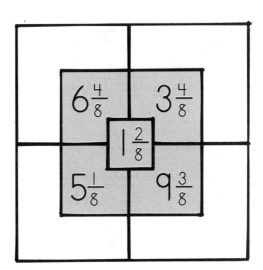

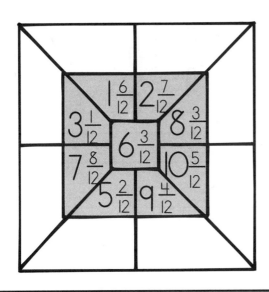

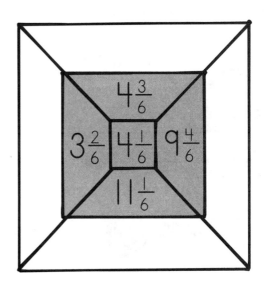

Name: _____

Fractions: Subtracting Mixed Numerals

A mixed numeral is a number written as a whole number and a fraction, such as 6 5/8.

Directions: Solve the problems. The first one is done for you.

$$7 \tfrac{3}{8}$$
$$-4 \tfrac{2}{8}$$
$$\overline{3 \tfrac{1}{8}}$$

$$4 \tfrac{5}{6}$$
$$-3 \tfrac{1}{6}$$

$$4 \tfrac{1}{2}$$
$$-3$$

$$7 \tfrac{5}{8}$$
$$-6 \tfrac{3}{8}$$

$$6 \tfrac{6}{8}$$
$$-1 \tfrac{1}{8}$$

$$5 \tfrac{3}{4}$$
$$-1 \tfrac{1}{4}$$

$$5 \tfrac{2}{3}$$
$$-3 \tfrac{1}{3}$$

$$4 \tfrac{8}{10}$$
$$-3 \tfrac{3}{10}$$

$$9 \tfrac{8}{9}$$
$$-4 \tfrac{3}{9}$$

$$7 \tfrac{2}{3}$$
$$-6 \tfrac{1}{3}$$

$$7 \tfrac{2}{3}$$
$$-5$$

$$9 \tfrac{8}{10}$$
$$-6 \tfrac{3}{10}$$

$$4 \tfrac{7}{9}$$
$$-2$$

$$6 \tfrac{7}{8}$$
$$-5 \tfrac{3}{8}$$

$$6 \tfrac{3}{4}$$
$$-3 \tfrac{1}{4}$$

$$5 \tfrac{6}{7}$$
$$-3 \tfrac{1}{7}$$

$$7 \tfrac{6}{7}$$
$$-2 \tfrac{4}{7}$$

Sally needs 1 3/8 yards of cloth to make a dress. She has 4 5/8 yards. How much will be left over?

_____

Name: _____

Fractions: Equivalent

Equivalent fractions name the same number, such as 1/2 and 2/4.

Directions: Study the example. Draw a line between the equivalent fractions in each row.

Example:
Equivalent fractions are equal to each other.

$$1/2 = 2/4 = 4/8$$

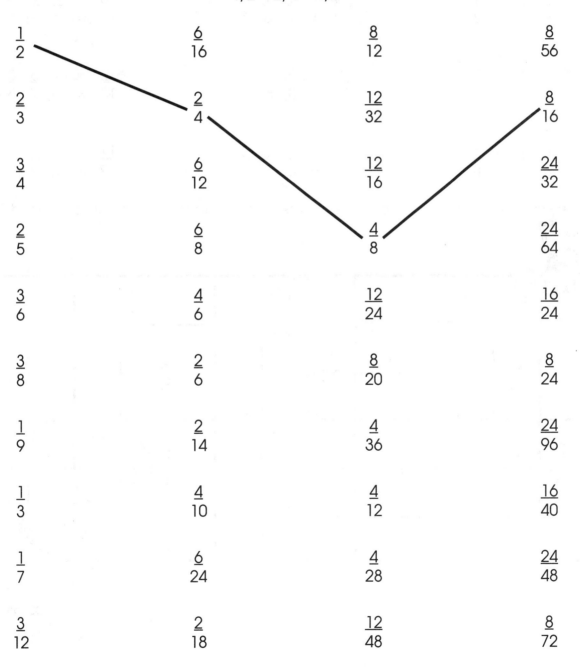

$\frac{1}{2}$	$\frac{6}{16}$	$\frac{8}{12}$	$\frac{8}{56}$
$\frac{2}{3}$	$\frac{2}{4}$	$\frac{12}{32}$	$\frac{8}{16}$
$\frac{3}{4}$	$\frac{6}{12}$	$\frac{12}{16}$	$\frac{24}{32}$
$\frac{2}{5}$	$\frac{6}{8}$	$\frac{4}{8}$	$\frac{24}{64}$
$\frac{3}{6}$	$\frac{4}{6}$	$\frac{12}{24}$	$\frac{16}{24}$
$\frac{3}{8}$	$\frac{2}{6}$	$\frac{8}{20}$	$\frac{8}{24}$
$\frac{1}{9}$	$\frac{2}{14}$	$\frac{4}{36}$	$\frac{24}{96}$
$\frac{1}{3}$	$\frac{4}{10}$	$\frac{4}{12}$	$\frac{16}{40}$
$\frac{1}{7}$	$\frac{6}{24}$	$\frac{4}{28}$	$\frac{24}{48}$
$\frac{3}{12}$	$\frac{2}{18}$	$\frac{12}{48}$	$\frac{8}{72}$

Name: _____

Fractions: Reducing

Reducing a fraction means to find the greatest common factor and divide.

Directions: Reduce each fraction. Circle the answer.

Example: $\dfrac{5}{15} = \dfrac{1}{3}$ factors of 5:   1, 5 $5 \div 5 = 1$
                 factors of 15:   1, 3, 5, 15 $15 \div 5 = 3$

$\dfrac{2}{4} = \dfrac{1}{2}, \dfrac{1}{6}, \dfrac{1}{8}$ $\dfrac{3}{9} = \dfrac{1}{6}, \dfrac{1}{3}, \dfrac{3}{6}$ $\dfrac{5}{10} = \dfrac{1}{5}, \dfrac{1}{2}, \dfrac{5}{6}$

$\dfrac{4}{12} = \dfrac{1}{4}, \dfrac{1}{3}, \dfrac{2}{3}$ $\dfrac{10}{15} = \dfrac{2}{3}, \dfrac{2}{5}, \dfrac{2}{7}$ $\dfrac{12}{14} = \dfrac{1}{8}, \dfrac{6}{7}, \dfrac{3}{5}$

$\dfrac{3}{24} = \dfrac{2}{12}, \dfrac{3}{6}, \dfrac{1}{8}$ $\dfrac{1}{11} = \dfrac{1}{11}, \dfrac{2}{5}, \dfrac{3}{4}$ $\dfrac{11}{22} = \dfrac{1}{12}, \dfrac{1}{2}, \dfrac{2}{5}$

Directions: Find the way home. Color the boxes with fractions equivalent to 1/8 and 1/3.

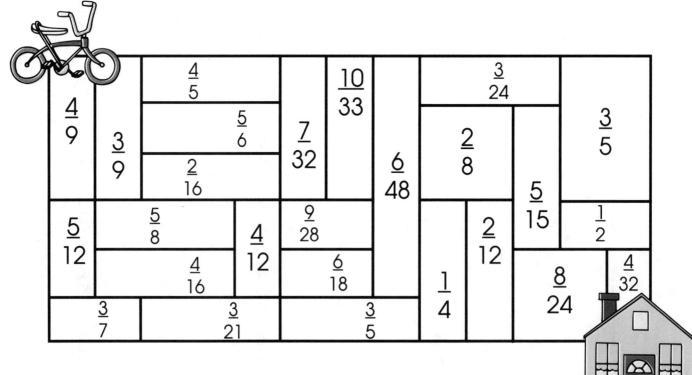

Name: _____

Fractions: Mixed Numerals

A mixed numeral is a number written as a whole number and a fraction, such as 6 5/8.

Directions: Change each fraction to a mixed numeral. Make the mixed numerals into fractions.

Example:

To change a fraction into a mixed numeral, divide the denominator (bottom number) into the numerator (top number). Put the remainder over the denominator.

To change a mixed numeral into a fraction, multiply the denominator by the whole number, add the numerator, and place it on top of the denominator.

$$\frac{14}{6} = 2\frac{2}{6} \qquad \begin{array}{r} 2\ r2 \\ 6\overline{)14} \\ \underline{12} \\ 2 \end{array}$$

$$3\frac{1}{7} = \frac{22}{7} \qquad (7 \times 3) + 1 = \frac{22}{7}$$

$$\frac{21}{6} = \underline{\quad}$$

$$\frac{24}{5} = \underline{\quad}$$

$$\frac{10}{3} = \underline{\quad}$$

$$\frac{21}{4} = \underline{\quad}$$

$$\frac{11}{6} = \underline{\quad}$$

$$\frac{13}{4} = \underline{\quad}$$

$$\frac{12}{5} = \underline{\quad}$$

$$\frac{10}{9} = \underline{\quad}$$

$$4\frac{3}{8} = \frac{\square}{8}$$

$$2\frac{1}{3} = \frac{\square}{3}$$

$$4\frac{3}{5} = \frac{\square}{5}$$

$$3\frac{4}{6} = \frac{\square}{6}$$

$$7\frac{1}{4} = \frac{\square}{4}$$

$$2\frac{3}{5} = \frac{\square}{5}$$

$$7\frac{1}{2} = \frac{\square}{2}$$

$$6\frac{5}{7} = \frac{\square}{7}$$

$$\frac{11}{8} = \underline{\quad}$$

$$\frac{21}{4} = \underline{\quad}$$

$$\frac{33}{5} = \underline{\quad}$$

$$\frac{13}{6} = \underline{\quad}$$

$$\frac{23}{7} = \underline{\quad}$$

$$8\frac{1}{3} = \underline{\quad}$$

$$9\frac{3}{7} = \underline{\quad}$$

$$\frac{32}{24} = \underline{\quad}$$

Name: _____

Review

Directions: Add or subtract the fractions and mixed numerals.

$\dfrac{3}{8} - \dfrac{1}{8} =$ ___ $\dfrac{3}{4} - \dfrac{2}{4} =$ ___ $\dfrac{3}{5} + \dfrac{1}{5} =$ ___ $\dfrac{4}{12} + \dfrac{3}{12} =$ ___ $\dfrac{3}{9} + \dfrac{1}{9} =$ ___

$$3\dfrac{1}{8} \\ +1\dfrac{3}{8}$$ $$4\dfrac{5}{6} \\ -3\dfrac{1}{6}$$ $$7\dfrac{5}{11} \\ +3\dfrac{3}{11}$$ $$8\dfrac{3}{9} \\ +2\dfrac{5}{9}$$ $$4\dfrac{7}{8} \\ -2\dfrac{5}{8}$$

Directions: Reduce the fractions. Circle the answers.

$\dfrac{3}{6} =$	$\dfrac{1}{7}$	$\dfrac{1}{2}$	$\dfrac{1}{4}$	$\dfrac{2}{8} =$	$\dfrac{1}{3}$	$\dfrac{1}{4}$	$\dfrac{1}{16}$	$\dfrac{4}{6} =$	$\dfrac{1}{4}$	$\dfrac{2}{3}$	$\dfrac{3}{9}$
$\dfrac{4}{20} =$	$\dfrac{1}{4}$	$\dfrac{1}{3}$	$\dfrac{1}{5}$	$\dfrac{7}{21} =$	$\dfrac{1}{7}$	$\dfrac{1}{3}$	$\dfrac{1}{5}$	$\dfrac{9}{12} =$	$\dfrac{3}{5}$	$\dfrac{1}{8}$	$\dfrac{3}{4}$

Directions: Reduce the fractions.

$\dfrac{6}{24} =$ ____ $\dfrac{8}{32} =$ ____ $\dfrac{2}{4} =$ ____

$\dfrac{3}{15} =$ ____ $\dfrac{6}{12} =$ ____ $\dfrac{3}{9} =$ ____

Directions: Change the mixed numerals to fractions and the fractions to mixed numerals.

$3\dfrac{1}{3} = \dfrac{\boxed{}}{3}$ $\dfrac{14}{4} =$ ____ $\dfrac{26}{6} =$ ____ $3\dfrac{7}{12} = \dfrac{\boxed{}}{12}$ $\dfrac{22}{7} =$ ____